TRUMPET 1

CANADIAN BRASS

Wedding Essentials

CONTENTS

This book is arranged for 2 B-flat trumpets, French horn, trombone, and tuba. The music in this book is from the personal library of Canadian Brass and has been performed and recorded by Canadian Brass.

Other books from Canadian Brass

Book of Beginning Quintets

Book of Easy Quintets

Book of Favorite Quintets (intermediate)

Book of Advanced Quintets

On Broadway

Rodgers and Hammerstein

Play Along with Canadian Brass (easy level)

Play Along with Canadian Brass (intermediate)

Canadian Brass Christmas Carols

Hymns for Brass

Immortal Folksongs

Favorite Classics

Visit *www.canadianbrass.com* for recordings from Canadian Brass

HAL•LEONARD®

CORPORATION

7777 W. BLUEMOUND RD. P.O. BOX 13819 MILWAUKEE, WI 53213

Visit Hal Leonard online at
www.halleonard.com

"AIR"
from *Water Music*

Handel
(1685–1759)
Arranged by Walter Barnes

LARGO

From *Xerxes*

1st B♭ CORNET/TRUMPET

George Frideric Handel
(1685-1759)
arranged by Walter Barnes

PRAYER
From *Hansel and Gretel*

1st TRUMPET

Engelbert Humperdinck
(1854-1921)
arranged by Henry Charles Smith

AIR ON THE G STRING
from Suite No. 3

**1st B♭ Trumpet
(Picc.)**

For shorter version, play 1st section (m. 1-5 and 2nd ending) once without piccolo trumpet.
Then 2nd section (m. 8-19) once with piccolo doubling trumpet in octaves.

J. S. Bach
(1685–1750)
Trans. by A. Frackenpohl

CANON

Johann Pachelbel
(1653-1706)
arranged by Walter Barnes

1st Bb CORNET/TRUMPET

FANFARE FROM ORPHEO

1st B♭ Trumpet

Claudio Monteverdi
(1567-1643)
adapted and arranged by Stephen McNeff

TRUMPET TUNE AND AYRE

Henry Purcell
(1659-1695)
arranged by Walter Barnes

1st B♭ CORNET/TRUMPET

TRUMPET VOLUNTARY

Stanley
(1713-1786)
arranged by Walter Barnes

Trumpet Voluntary *continued*

TRUMPET VOLUNTARY

Jeremiah Clarke
(1673-1707)
arranged by Walter Barnes

1st B♭ CORNET/TRUMPET

BRIDAL CHORUS
from LOHENGRIN

Richard Wagner
(1813-1883)
edited by Canadian Brass

1st B♭ Trumpet

WEDDING MARCH

1st B♭ Trumpet

Felix Mendelssohn
(1809–1847)
Adapted by Ryan Anthony

RONDEAU

(Theme from *Masterpiece Theatre*)

Jean-Joseph Mouret
(1682-1738)
arranged by Walter Barnes

1st B♭ CORNET/TRUMPET

ALBASON FANFARE

Gottfried Reiche (1667-1734)

Trumpet in B-Flat

Trumpet in B-Flat - Alternate Key

Piccolo Trumpet in A - Original Key